Little Big Giant

Stories of Wisdom and Inspiration

Introduction

As the sun set over the bustling streets of Florence, a young Galileo Galilei stood in awe, gazing up at the night sky. His mind raced with questions and curiosity, as he watched the stars twinkle and dance above him. Little did he know, this moment would ignite a passion for astronomy and science that would change the course of history. From his groundbreaking discoveries of the moons of Jupiter to his infamous clash with the Catholic Church, Galileo's life was a rollercoaster of triumphs and challenges. But through it all, he remained steadfast in his pursuit of knowledge, forever leaving his mark on the world as one of the greatest scientific minds of all time.

Table of Contents

Table of Contents **5**

Chapter 1 **7**

Early Life and Education 7

Chapter 2 **15**

First Discoveries and Inventions 15

Chapter 3 **23**

Conflict with the Church 23

Chapter 4 **31**

The Telescope and Observations of the Sky 31

Chapter 5 **39**

The Theory of Heliocentrism 39

Chapter 6 **47**

Trial and Imprisonment 47

Chapter 7 **55**

Continued Scientific Discoveries 55

Chapter 8 **63**

Legacy and Influence 63

Chapter 9   **71**

Personal Life and Relationships   71

Chapter 10   **79**

Impact on Modern Science and Technology   79

Chapter 1

Early Life and Education

Galileo Galilei was born on February 15, 1564 in Pisa, Italy. He was the first of six children born to Vincenzo Galilei, a musician, and Giulia Ammannati. From a young age, Galileo showed a strong curiosity and love for learning. He was always asking questions and seeking answers to satisfy his curious mind.

As a child, Galileo was homeschooled by his father who taught him mathematics and music. He excelled in both subjects and showed a natural talent for numbers and equations. His father also introduced him to the works of ancient Greek philosophers, which sparked Galileo's interest in science.

At the age of 10, Galileo and his family moved to Florence, where he attended a local monastery school. Here, he continued to excel in mathematics and music, but also developed an interest in astronomy. He would often spend hours gazing at the stars and planets, wondering about their movements and patterns.

When Galileo was 17, he enrolled at the University of Pisa to study medicine, as his father wanted him to become a doctor. However, Galileo's true passion was in mathematics and science, and he spent most of his time studying these subjects instead of medicine. He even conducted his own experiments, such as dropping objects from the top of the Leaning Tower of Pisa to test the laws of gravity.

Despite his lack of interest in medicine, Galileo graduated from the university in 1584 with a degree in mathematics. He then returned to Florence and began teaching mathematics at the university. He quickly gained a reputation as a brilliant teacher and scientist.

Key Takeaway: Galileo's early life and education played a crucial role in shaping him into the renowned scientist he would become. His curiosity, love for learning, and natural talent for mathematics and science set him on the path to discovering groundbreaking theories and inventions.

Chapter 2

First Discoveries and Inventions

Galileo Galilei was a curious and determined young man. He was always fascinated by the world around him and loved to ask questions. When he was just a young boy, he would often spend hours staring at the night sky, wondering about the stars and planets.

As he grew older, Galileo's passion for science and discovery only grew stronger. He began to conduct experiments and make observations that would change the course of history. In this chapter, we will explore some of Galileo's first discoveries and inventions.

The Telescope

One of Galileo's most famous inventions was the telescope. He was not the first person to create a telescope, but he was the first to use it for scientific purposes. Galileo made his own telescope using a tube, lenses, and a wooden frame. With this simple invention, he was able to see things that no one had ever seen before.

Galileo pointed his telescope towards the night sky and was amazed by what he saw. He discovered that the moon was not a smooth, perfect sphere as many people believed, but it had craters and mountains. He also observed that the Milky Way was made up of countless stars and that there were four moons orbiting around Jupiter.

These discoveries were groundbreaking and challenged the beliefs of the time. Galileo's telescope helped him prove that the Earth was not the center of the universe, as many people believed, but that it revolved around the sun.

The Pendulum Clock

Aside from the telescope, Galileo also invented the pendulum clock. Before his invention, clocks were not very accurate and would often lose or gain time. Galileo's pendulum clock used the swinging motion of a pendulum to keep time accurately. This invention was a huge improvement in timekeeping and is still used in clocks today.

Key Takeaway: Galileo's telescope and pendulum clock were important inventions that helped him make groundbreaking discoveries and advancements in science. These inventions also paved the way for future inventions and technologies.

In Conclusion

Galileo Galilei's curiosity and determination led him to make incredible discoveries and inventions that changed the way we understand the world. His telescope and pendulum clock were just the beginning of his many contributions to science. In the next chapter, we will explore more of Galileo's discoveries and how they shaped our understanding of the universe.

Chapter 3

Conflict with the Church

Galileo Galilei had always been fascinated by the stars and the secrets they held. He spent countless hours gazing at the night sky, wondering about the mysteries of the universe. As he grew older, his curiosity only intensified and he began to question the teachings of the Church.

At the time, the Church had a strong hold on society and any ideas that went against their beliefs were considered heresy. Galileo's theories and observations about the Earth and the planets went against the Church's teachings and they saw him as a threat.

One of Galileo's most controversial ideas was that the Earth was not the center of the universe, but rather it revolved around the sun. This went against the Church's belief that the Earth was the center of God's creation. Galileo's findings were also in direct conflict with the Bible, which the Church believed to be the ultimate truth.

Despite the Church's disapproval, Galileo continued to share his theories and findings with the public. He wrote books and gave lectures, gaining a following of people who were fascinated by his ideas. However, this only angered the Church even more.

In 1616, Galileo was summoned to Rome by the Church to defend his beliefs. He was accused of heresy and was forced to recant his theories. He was also forbidden from teaching or writing about his ideas in the future.

But Galileo could not stay silent. He continued to study and observe the universe, and his findings only solidified his beliefs. In 1632, he published a book called "Dialogue Concerning the Two Chief World Systems" which compared the geocentric (Earth-centered) and heliocentric (sun-centered) models of the universe. This book was seen as a direct attack on the Church's teachings and Galileo was once again summoned to Rome.

This time, the Church was not as forgiving. Galileo was put on trial and found guilty of heresy. He was sentenced to house arrest for the rest of his life and his books were banned. Galileo's health deteriorated and he spent his final years confined to his home, but his ideas continued to spread and inspire future scientists.

Key Takeaway: Galileo's conflict with the Church teaches us the importance of questioning and challenging beliefs. It also shows the dangers of suppressing new ideas and the importance of open-mindedness and freedom of thought.

Chapter 4

The Telescope and Observations of the Sky

Galileo Galilei was a curious man, always seeking to learn more about the world around him. He had already made groundbreaking discoveries in the field of physics and mathematics, but he was not satisfied. Galileo wanted to know more about the sky and the stars that twinkled above.

One day, while walking through the streets of Venice, Galileo came across a shop selling lenses. He was immediately intrigued and purchased a few to experiment with. Using his knowledge of optics, Galileo was able to create a device that could magnify objects from a distance. This was the birth of the telescope.

Galileo's telescope was not like the ones we have today. It was made of a simple tube with two lenses at either end. But this simple invention changed the way people saw the world. With his telescope, Galileo was able to see things that were too far away for the naked eye to see. He could see the craters on the moon, the rings of Saturn, and the moons of Jupiter.

Galileo was fascinated by what he saw through his telescope. He spent countless nights observing the sky, making detailed notes and sketches of what he saw. He even discovered that the Milky Way was made up of countless stars, contrary to the popular belief at the time that it was just a cloudy band in the sky.

But not everyone was as excited about Galileo's discoveries as he was. The Catholic Church, which had a lot of influence in those times, did not agree with Galileo's findings. They believed that the Earth was the center of the universe and all other planets revolved around it. Galileo's observations challenged this belief and caused controversy.

Despite facing opposition, Galileo continued to observe the sky and make new discoveries. He even discovered the phases of Venus, which further proved that the Earth was not the center of the universe. His telescope had opened up a whole new world of knowledge and understanding.

Key Takeaway: Galileo's telescope allowed him to see things that were invisible to the naked eye, and his observations challenged the beliefs of his time. It is important to always question and seek answers, even if they go against

popular beliefs.

Chapter 5

The Theory of Heliocentrism

Galileo Galilei was a brilliant scientist who lived in the 16th and 17th century. He was known for his groundbreaking discoveries and theories, one of which was the theory of heliocentrism. This theory changed the way people viewed the universe and is still relevant in our understanding of space today.

Before Galileo's time, people believed that the Earth was the center of the universe and that all other celestial bodies revolved around it. This was known as the geocentric theory. However, Galileo had a different idea. He believed that the Sun was actually the center of the universe and that the Earth and other planets revolved around it. This theory is known as heliocentrism.

Galileo's theory was met with a lot of resistance and criticism from the church and other scientists. They believed that the geocentric theory was the truth and that Galileo's ideas were wrong and even heretical. But Galileo was determined to prove his theory and he used his skills as an astronomer to gather evidence.

He observed the movements of the planets and stars through his telescope and recorded his findings. He also studied the work of other astronomers, such as Nicolaus Copernicus, who had also proposed the heliocentric theory. Galileo's observations and research provided strong evidence to support his theory.

Despite facing many challenges, Galileo continued to share his ideas and findings with the world. He wrote a book called "Dialogue Concerning the Two Chief World Systems" where he explained his theory in a way that was easy for people to understand. This book sparked a lot of controversy and eventually led to Galileo being put on trial by the church.

But even during his trial, Galileo remained steadfast in his belief in heliocentrism. He refused to recant his theory and was placed under house arrest for the rest of his life. However, his theory continued to spread and gain support, eventually becoming widely accepted as the truth.

Key Takeaway: Galileo's theory of heliocentrism was a major turning point in our understanding of the universe. It showed us that sometimes, new ideas and theories can challenge long-held beliefs and change the way we see the world. It also taught us the importance of standing up for what we believe in, even in the face of opposition.

Chapter 6

Trial and Imprisonment

Galileo Galilei was a man ahead of his time. He was a scientist, philosopher, and mathematician who made groundbreaking discoveries that changed the way we see the world. But his ideas were not always accepted by the people of his time.

In 1633, Galileo was put on trial by the Catholic Church for his belief in the heliocentric theory, which stated that the Earth revolved around the sun. This was in direct contradiction to the Church's teachings, which stated that the Earth was the center of the universe.

Galileo was brought before the Inquisition, a powerful court within the Catholic Church that dealt with matters of heresy. He was accused of spreading false teachings and was threatened with imprisonment if he did not recant his beliefs.

But Galileo refused to back down. He stood by his scientific discoveries and defended his beliefs with passion and conviction. He argued that his theories were based on observation and evidence, not on blind faith.

Despite his best efforts, Galileo was found guilty and sentenced to house arrest for the rest of his life. This was a harsh punishment for a man who had dedicated his life to the pursuit of knowledge and truth.

During his imprisonment, Galileo continued to write and study, even though he was not allowed to publish his work. He wrote letters to his friends and fellow scientists, discussing his theories and ideas. He also continued to correspond with his daughter, who was a source of comfort and support during this difficult time.

Galileo's imprisonment did not break his spirit. He remained determined to share his knowledge and ideas with the world, even if it meant facing consequences from the Church.

Key Takeaway: Galileo's trial and imprisonment show us the importance of standing up for what we believe in, even in the face of opposition. It also teaches us the value of perseverance and determination in the pursuit of knowledge and truth.

Chapter 7

Continued Scientific Discoveries

Galileo Galilei was a man on a mission. After his groundbreaking discoveries about the moons of Jupiter and the phases of Venus, he was determined to continue his exploration of the universe. He believed that there were still many secrets waiting to be uncovered, and he was determined to be the one to uncover them.

Galileo spent countless hours in his observatory, studying the stars and planets.

He used his telescope to observe the moon, and he was amazed by the intricate details he could see. He noticed that the moon's surface was not smooth, as many people had believed, but instead it was full of craters and mountains. Galileo also observed that the moon had phases, just like Venus, which further proved his theory that the planets revolved around the sun.

But Galileo's curiosity did not stop there. He turned his telescope towards the planet Saturn and was shocked to see that it had rings. He couldn't believe his eyes and spent hours studying the rings and trying to understand their composition. Galileo's observations of Saturn would later be confirmed by other scientists, solidifying his reputation as a brilliant astronomer.

Galileo's discoveries didn't just stop at the moon and Saturn. He also observed the sun and noticed dark spots on its surface. Through his observations, he concluded that the sun was not a perfect, unchanging sphere as previously believed, but instead it had imperfections just like the moon and other planets.

As Galileo continued his exploration of the universe, he faced opposition from those who did not believe in his findings. Some people believed that the Earth was the center of the universe and that everything revolved around it. Galileo's discoveries challenged this belief and caused controversy among the scientific community.

But Galileo was not deterred. He continued to make groundbreaking discoveries, including the discovery of sunspots and the moons of Saturn. His contributions to science were immense and helped shape our understanding of the universe.

Key Takeaway: Galileo Galilei's continued scientific discoveries proved that the Earth was not the center of the universe and that the planets revolved around the sun. His observations of the moon, Saturn, and the sun helped pave the way for future discoveries and solidified his place in history as one of the greatest scientists of all time.

Chapter 8

Legacy and Influence

Galileo Galilei was not only a brilliant scientist and mathematician, but he was also a man who left a lasting impact on the world. His discoveries and ideas have influenced many aspects of our lives today.

One of Galileo's greatest legacies is his contribution to the scientific method. He believed in using observation and experimentation to understand the world around us. This approach to science has become the foundation for modern scientific research and has led to countless discoveries and advancements.

Galileo's work in astronomy also left a lasting impact. His observations of the moon, planets, and stars challenged the widely accepted belief that the Earth was the center of the universe. His discoveries paved the way for future astronomers to continue exploring and learning about our vast universe.

But Galileo's influence was not limited to the field of science. His ideas and beliefs also had a significant impact on society. He believed in the power of reason and the importance of questioning authority. This challenged the traditional thinking of his time and sparked a revolution in thought that would eventually lead to the Age of Enlightenment.

Galileo's legacy can also be seen in the advancements in technology and engineering. His understanding of motion and gravity has been crucial in the development of modern transportation and infrastructure. Without his contributions, our world would look very different today.

Furthermore, Galileo's influence can still be felt in the way we view the world and ourselves. His teachings have encouraged us to question, explore, and think critically. He showed us that there is always more to discover and that we should never stop seeking knowledge.

Key Takeaway: Galileo Galilei's legacy and influence extend far beyond the scientific community. His ideas and discoveries have shaped our understanding of the world and continue to inspire us to question, explore, and innovate. He will always be remembered as a pioneer of the scientific method and a true visionary who changed the course of history.

Chapter 9

Personal Life and Relationships

Galileo Galilei was not just a brilliant scientist, but he also had a personal life filled with love and relationships. Despite his busy schedule and dedication to his work, Galileo made time for his family and friends.

Galileo was born into a large family, with six siblings. He was the eldest and often took on the responsibility of caring for his younger siblings. His father, Vincenzo Galilei, was a musician and wanted Galileo to follow in his footsteps. However, Galileo's passion for science and mathematics was evident from a young age.

As he grew older, Galileo fell in love with a woman named Marina Gamba. They had three children together, but unfortunately, they were not able to get married due to societal norms at the time. Despite this, Galileo loved Marina deeply and took care of her and their children.

Galileo also had a close relationship with his students and colleagues. He was a dedicated teacher and mentor, always willing to help others understand complex scientific concepts. He often invited his students to his home, where they would conduct experiments and discuss their findings.

One of Galileo's most significant relationships was with his dear friend, Prince Cesi. Prince Cesi was the founder of the Accademia dei Lincei, a prestigious scientific society in Rome. Galileo was a member of this society and often collaborated with Prince Cesi on various projects.

In addition to his personal relationships, Galileo also had a love for music. He played the lute and composed music in his free time. He believed that music and mathematics were closely related, and he often incorporated his knowledge of math into his musical compositions.

Despite his busy life, Galileo always made time for his loved ones. He enjoyed spending time with his family, playing music with his friends, and discussing scientific theories with his colleagues. His personal life was just as important to him as his work.

Key Takeaway: Galileo Galilei was not just a brilliant scientist, but he also had a rich personal life filled with love and relationships. He showed that it is possible to balance one's passions with personal connections, and that both are essential for a fulfilling life.

Chapter 10

Impact on Modern Science and Technology

Galileo Galilei's contributions to the world of science and technology are still felt today, centuries after his death. His discoveries and theories revolutionized the way we understand the universe and paved the way for modern scientific advancements. In this chapter, we will explore the lasting impact of Galileo's work on our world.

Galileo's most famous contribution to science was his support for the heliocentric theory, which stated that the Earth and other planets revolve around the sun. This challenged the widely accepted geocentric theory, which claimed that the Earth was the center of the universe. Galileo's observations and experiments with his telescope provided evidence for the heliocentric theory and changed the way we view our place in the solar system.

One of Galileo's most important discoveries was the four largest moons of Jupiter, now known as the Galilean moons. This observation further supported the heliocentric theory and also opened up the possibility of other planets having their own moons. Today, we know that our solar system is filled with countless moons, and Galileo's discovery was the first step in understanding their importance.

Galileo also made significant contributions to the field of physics. He conducted experiments with objects falling from different heights and discovered that they all fell at the same rate, regardless of their weight. This led to the development of the laws of motion and gravity, which are fundamental principles in modern physics.

In addition to his scientific discoveries, Galileo also invented many important tools and instruments. His improvements to the telescope allowed for more detailed observations of the night sky, and his design for the thermometer is still used today. Galileo also made advancements in the field of military technology, creating a military compass and a geometric and military compass.

Galileo's impact on modern science and technology cannot be overstated. His theories and discoveries laid the foundation for many of the scientific advancements we enjoy today. Without his contributions, our understanding of the universe and our ability to explore it would be greatly limited.

Key Takeaway: Galileo Galilei's work revolutionized the fields of astronomy, physics, and technology. His support for the heliocentric theory, discovery of Jupiter's moons, and inventions have had a lasting impact on modern science and continue to inspire new discoveries and advancements.

Dear Reader,

Thank you for choosing "Little Big Giant - Stories of Wisdom and Inspiration"! We hope this book has inspired and motivated you on your own journey to success.

If you enjoyed reading this book and believe in the power of its message, we kindly ask for your support. Please consider leaving a positive review on the platform where you purchased the book. Your review will help spread the message to more young readers, empowering them to dream big and achieve greatness. We acknowledge that mistakes can happen, and we appreciate your forgiveness.

Remember, the overall message of this book is the key. Thank you for being a part of our mission to inspire and uplift young minds.